HEROES AND V.

TWO PLAYS

Heroes and Villains

TWO PLAYS

Contents

CAMBRIDGE
UNIVERSITY PRESS

Cambridge Reading

General Editors
Richard Brown and Kate Ruttle

Consultant Editor
Jean Glasberg

PUBLISHED BY THE PRESS SYNDICATE OF THE UNIVERSITY OF CAMBRIDGE
The Pitt Building, Trumpington Street, Cambridge, United Kingdom

CAMBRIDGE UNIVERSITY PRESS
The Edinburgh Building, Cambridge CB2 2RU, UK   http://www.cup.cam.ac.uk
40 West 20th Street, New York, NY 10011–4211, USA   http://www.cup.org
10 Stamford Road, Oakleigh, Melbourne 3166, Australia
Ruiz de Alarcón 13, 28014 Madrid, Spain

Heroes and Villains: two plays
Whitney Snow
Text © Richard Brown 2000
Illustrations © Stella Voce 2000
Christmas in the Other House
Text © Judith O'Neill 2000
Illustrations © Gerry Ball 2000
Design by Angela Ashton

Adapted from the original stories in *Heroes and Villains*, edited by Tony Bradman,
published by Cambridge University Press, 1998 (ISBN 0521 57551 6)

First published 2000

Printed in the United Kingdom at the University Press, Cambridge

Typeface Concorde

A catalogue record for this book is available from the British Library

ISBN 0 521 66436 5 paperback

PERFORMANCE
For permission to give a public performance of *Whitney Snow* or
Christmas in the Other House, please write in the first instance to
Permissions Department, Cambridge University Press,
The Edinburgh Building, Shaftesbury Road, Cambridge CB2 2RU.

Whitney Snow

Richard Brown

Illustrated by Stella Voce

Contents

Introduction

This play has been written as a radio play.

If you are **reading** the play in a group, you may **double up** the parts, by giving one person two small parts to read. Parts marked with the same number are suitable for 'doubling up'.

If you are **recording** it as a radio play, you can use one actor per part or double up the parts. (Anyone playing more than one part, though, will need to make their voice sound different for each part, or people listening may get confused!) You will also need a sound effects person to produce all the sounds that occur through the play, e.g. telephones ringing. Look out for other opportunities to introduce sounds that will add atmosphere to the recording. For instance, at the end of scene 3 you could have the sound of scissors cutting Whitney's hair, and in scene 8 you could have the sound of shouting in the background.

If you do decide to stage the play, you will need to keep the stage sets very simple and to think carefully about scene changes. The play has a pantomime feel to it, so you could decide to draw that out in the way you perform it. The Narrator could stand to one side, commenting on the action; you might decide to cut the Narrator's lines that describe action that will be seen on stage. You will need someone to act the part of Wolfie (perhaps wearing a wolf mask). You will also need to use **extras** – actors who don't speak but who make scenes more life-like by being there, for example extra Henchmen and Dwarfs, and some Grannies and War Widows for the crowd scenes.

Characters

Whitney Snow	*princess*
Queenie	*her stepmother*
Dr Wright	*the palace doctor*
¹**Tom**	*a Dwarf*
²**Suzy**	*a Dwarf*
Red	*a grown-up Red Riding Hood*
³**Goldie**	*a grown-up Goldilocks*
³**Henchman**	
²**Maid**	
Narrator	
¹**Computer**	

Scene 1

Palace Tower, evening

Narrator Queenie, the wicked queen of the city, looked out of the window of her top-floor flat at Palace Tower. She watched her hated stepdaughter, Whitney Snow, in the courtyard below.

Queenie What's that idiot Henchman doing? *Bowing* to her? I'll have him slung in the dungeons. I'm the only one around here they should bow to – don't they know that by now? Or has she turned their heads? She's got ten times worse since her father went off to the Wars. Sullen. Stuck up. And silly. I've had enough of it. Pah! Something'll have to be done about Whitney Snow, princess or no princess.

Queenie (*Turning to her computer*) Computer. Who is the fairest of them all?

Computer Whitney Snow, I'm afraid, Your Majesty.

Queenie (*Crossly*) Don't you ever change your tune? Computer, who is the most cunning of them all?

Computer You are, most gracious queen.

Queenie It's a good job you said that, Computer. But why should *she* always be the fairest? Just because she's younger. It's an insult. I've had enough of it. I'm going to have to get rid of her. My lovely

collection of poisons should help me do that.
Now, let me see, which one would be best?
Ah, this one! That should send her out of her
mind. This is going to be fun! Then we'll soon see
who's the fairest around here.

Scene 2

Later that night

Maid   Here's your nightcap, Ma'am. I'll just take Whitney's –

Queenie   No, ask her in here, to drink it with me.

Maid   (*Surprised*) Yes, Ma'am.

Queenie   Off you go, then, scarper. (***Maid** exits*) Which mug shall I put the poison in? She's bound to suspect me – I've never offered her a nightcap before. But, then, who is the most cunning of them all? I'll put the poison in *my* mug. She's too clever by half; she's bound to take that instead of her own.

                    ***Whitney** enters.*

Queenie   Whitney, my dear! I thought you'd like to join me for a nightcap.

Whitney   (*Suspicious*) Your Majesty, you shouldn't have.

Queenie   Such a nice change, don't you think? Here it is. Nice hot milk. Drink it up quickly now, dear.

Narrator   Whitney only took a few cautious sips, but that was enough. Her eyes began to roll, her limbs twitched and danced; soon she was raving. Within a few minutes, she was shouting and cowering and running about in all directions, as if she was being pursued by a horrible creature.

Queenie	(*Gleefully*) Oh, wonderful! Just look at her. There's nothing pretty about her now!
Whitney	Help me! What's happening? My head's on fire.
Queenie	Maybe I should publish a book of poison recipes. *Poisons for All Occasions*. It's bound to be a bestseller!
Whitney	There's a monster after me. Help!
Queenie	Aren't you feeling well, dear? I'll call the doctor.
Narrator	Dr Wright's surgery was on the seventeenth floor. When he heard Queenie's voice and, worse, what the problem was, he began to panic. He couldn't find his medical bag (it eventually turned up under a copy of *Grimm News*), then he got lost in the endless corridors, and the lift got stuck. The maid met him outside Queenie's apartment.
Maid	(*Keeping her voice low*) Everything all right, Doctor?
Doctor	(*Breathless*) Yes, thank you. I'm just a little puffed out.
Maid	It's your first day, isn't it?
Doctor	Oh, yes. Don't remind me. I spent most of the morning riding up and down in the lift, looking for my surgery. No-one seemed to know where it was.

Maid	That's because Queenie moved it when the last doctor died.
Doctor	Died? What of?
Maid	Oops! Said enough already. Just watch your back, Doc. OK?
Doctor	Well, I must see to my patient.
Maid	Have you seen the princess yet?
Doctor	Yes, isn't she . . . ? I mean, she's so beautiful.
Maid	Sad, too, poor thing.
Doctor	Sad? What about?
Maid	Her father going off to the Wars, leaving the queen in charge. She really misses him. Anyway, the queen says Whitney's not feeling well. You'd better go in. And, Doctor –
Doctor	Yes?
Maid	Good luck!

*The **doctor** enters Queenie's flat.*

Queenie	Ah, Doctor! You took your time! My stepdaughter – I think she's gone mad. Look!

Doctor   I'm so sorry, Your Majesty.

Narrator   He tried to approach Whitney as she crouched in a corner, but the princess hissed at him.

Doctor   This is most distressing.

Queenie   (*Pretending to cry*) Yes, I'm quite heartbroken.

Doctor   Has she shown signs of madness before?

Queenie   She might have. She's always been highly strung.

Doctor   Does madness run in the family?

Narrator   Queenie glared at him, and then remembered that Whitney was only her stepdaughter.

Queenie   Yes, that must be it, I'm sure.

Doctor   (*Searching in his bag*) I'll prescribe some medicine to calm her.

Queenie   No need for that, Doctor. I've sent for a strait-jacket.

Doctor   (*Aghast*) You've done what?

Queenie   Well, you can see she's dangerous.

Doctor   Yes, but I can't believe . . . It's so cruel.

Queenie	Just look at her! She's like a wild animal.
Doctor	Yes, but it might be temporary. Something she's eaten.
Narrator	Two Henchmen burst in with a strait-jacket. With some difficulty, they trussed Whitney up.
Doctor	(*Distressed*) Oh, this is terrible.
Queenie	Stop blubbering, man. You're a doctor, aren't you?
Doctor	Of course, but –
Queenie	Put her in the isolation ward immediately. See that no-one but you goes near her. I will supply you with all the medicine you'll need. See that she takes it. *Or else.*
Doctor	(*Intimidated*) Of course, Your Majesty.
Narrator	The Henchmen took Whitney down to the doctor's surgery, and he followed them, sorely troubled by what had happened.
Queenie	Computer, *now* who is the fairest of them all?
Computer	You are, Your Majesty.
Queenie	Yes! (*She claps her hands with glee*) Computer, just out of interest, tell me also – who is the most cunning of them all?

Computer   You are, Your Majesty.

Queenie   Of course I am, you fool. *I'm* not mad, am I?

Narrator   Queenie danced triumphantly around the room, kicking up her skinny legs.

Scene 3

Dr Wright's surgery, two days later

Narrator At last, Dr Wright had managed to remove Whitney's strait-jacket. She was now sleeping.

Maid She's looking ever so much better, isn't she, Doctor?

Doctor It's such a relief, I can tell you.

Maid Did you find out what was wrong?

Doctor (*Lowers his voice*) She was poisoned.

Maid (*Aghast*) No! Really? Who by?

Doctor Who do you think?

Maid Does her name begin with 'Q'?

Doctor How did you guess? Anyway, I was able to make an antidote.

Maid You are clever, Doctor. How did you find out about the poison?

Doctor Whitney always resisted taking the queen's medicine; she hated it. So I put a drop of it under the microscope. As soon as the computer told me it was poison, I understood everything.

Maid Everything?

Doctor	Yes, why you're all so frightened to raise your voice around here. Why everyone is scared of their own shadow. What the queen is *really* like. And the danger Whitney is in. This is a terrible place.
Maid	Talk like that, Doctor, and you'll get thrown into the dungeons.
Doctor	If you know what it's like here, I wonder why you stay.
Maid	We have no choice. There are Henchmen on the door. And the queen has surveillance cameras everywhere outside. Besides, we're waiting for the king to return from the Wars, when everything will get back to normal.
	Maid exits.
Doctor	Whitney! Wake up. Please.
Whitney	(*Waking up*) I feel – oh, almost myself again. I'm not burning up inside any more. And those demons in my head – they've gone! It's wonderful!
Doctor	I'm so pleased. I was very worried.
Whitney	I think I owe you my life, Doctor.
Doctor	(*Stammering*) Oh, that's nothing. Just doing my job. Here, let me help you up.

Whitney	Thank you Doctor. It wasn't 'nothing'. What happened to me?
Doctor	(*Whispers*) Your stepmother poisoned you.
Whitney	(*Horrified*) Are you sure? How? It was in the nightcap, wasn't it? What a fool I was to drink it! You're right, she just wants me out of the way.
Doctor	I still find it hard to believe.
Whitney	I don't. She's gone too far this time. I knew she was wicked, and jealous, and cunning. But this? This is something different.
Doctor	Whitney, you're in grave danger here. You must get away before she tries it again.
Whitney	(*Indignant*) But this is my home! My father's! *She* should leave.
Doctor	Shh! Keep your voice down. We've got to let her think you're still ill, while we plan what to do.
Whitney	Wait till my father hears about this. But until then . . . Yes, I will have to escape.
Doctor	I don't think you have much of a choice. Have you anywhere you can go?
Whitney	No, I've always lived in the palace. But I'll find somewhere. Anywhere. You'll have to go into hiding too, Doctor, until they stop looking for you.

Doctor	Of course. I'll go with you.
Whitney	No. You've already risked your life for me. I cannot ask for more.
Doctor	But –
Whitney	Don't worry. I can look after myself. I'll be all right. We'll keep in touch by mobile, right? Now, there's something I want you to do for me before we leave.
Doctor	Anything. What is it?
Whitney	Cut my hair.
Doctor	What? Your beautiful golden hair? I couldn't.
Whitney	It's too well known. It's sure to give me away. You'll have to. Here are the scissors. Now, be brave, Doctor, and cut!
Narrator	A little later, disguised as a maid and with her hair cropped, Whitney slipped out of Palace Tower unrecognised. Dr Wright left too, going his own way.
Whitney	(*Angrily*) I'll be back one day, Queenie – that's a promise. And then you'll be on your knees begging for mercy. Just you wait and see!

Scene 4

Midnight in the city, that night

Narrator   Whitney wandered through the streets, looking for somewhere to stay where the queen's spies wouldn't find her.

Whitney   (*To herself*) It's wonderful to be free again. To think I haven't been allowed outside the palace since my father left. *She* always kept me prisoner . . . Everything looks so different at night.

Narrator   Suddenly, she turned a corner and saw one of the queen's henchmen bullying a dwarf.

Henchman   You scrawny little toad. You dozy bit of dung. Thought you could slide by me unseen, did you? (*Pulls **Tom**'s beard*)

Tom   Ouch! Let me go.

Henchman   Not until you tell me what you're doing slinking around here at night, you horrible little worm! (*Tugs harder on the beard*)

Tom   OUCH! LET ME GO!

Whitney   (*Marching up to **Henchman**, outraged*) How dare you! Leave that Dwarf alone AT ONCE.

Henchman   (*Surprised, letting go of **Tom***) Who the devil . . . ? And what's the little sprat to you?

Whitney   (*Deciding to use flattery to disarm him*) Come here. Let me whisper something in your ear. (**Henchman** *approaches*) You are the queen's man. It makes me sad to think of you having to soil your hands with such . . . such people as this silly little Dwarf.

Henchman   Oh, but –

Whitney   No, I mean it. I do so admire what you do. So strong and handsome.

Henchman   (*Abashed*) Handsome? Me?

Whitney   So modest too! Look, I spoke hastily to you just now. Let me make it up to you. Close your eyes and count to a hundred, and I'll give you a kiss to say I'm sorry.

Henchman   You will? Oh, this is my lucky day. (*Eyes closed, begins to count*)

Whitney   (*Whispers*) Time to scarper, Dwarfie. Come on.

Narrator   Whitney and Tom ran off and didn't stop until they were well out of sight.

Tom   (*Puffed out*) That was terrific. Brave. Fantastic! I can't begin to thank you.

Whitney   I never did like bullying. I'm Whitney Snow, by the way. What's your name?

Tom	Tom.
Whitney	Well, nice to meet you, Tom. Now, I'm going to ask you a favour in return, if you don't mind. I've got nowhere to go tonight. My stepmother, the queen –
Tom	(*Startled*) The queen?
Whitney	Yes, sorry, I should have explained. I'm running away from her. That's why I'm in disguise. I'm not really a maid, you know.
Tom	Of course. You're the *princess*! I wondered where I'd seen you before. You must come back with me to White Tower. That's where all the Dwarfs live. You'll be safe there. And don't worry, we have ways of keeping the Henchmen at bay.
Whitney	Are you sure? That'd be wonderful. I've often looked across the city to White Tower and wondered what it was like there.

Scene 5

Palace Tower, the next day

Queenie   (*To herself*) With Whitney out of the way, I should be feeling happy. And I am. But I sense something strange in the air. I can't see anything out of the ordinary on my surveillance screens, but *something* is happening, I feel sure. I wonder if those stupid Henchmen are keeping something from me . . . I'll see what my computer has to say. Computer, who is the fairest of them all?

Computer   Whitney Snow, Your Majesty.

Queenie   *What?* I don't believe it! She looked like a demented bat when I last saw her. Now think carefully before you answer, Computer. Who is the brightest of them all?

Computer   Whitney Snow, Your Majesty.

Queenie   (*Outraged*) How dare you! . . . Unless . . . There's something fishy going on here. What has that dumb doctor been up to? Has he been stupid enough to make her better? (*Shouts*) HENCHMAN!

Henchman   (*Running in*) Yes, Your Majesty?

Queenie   Where is my stepdaughter? Where is the doctor?

Henchman (*Stutters with fear*) They've escaped, Your Majesty.

Queenie *Escaped!* You've let them go? Aahhh! You fool! Idiot! Get down into the dungeons at once and lock yourself in.

Henchman (*Trembling*) Yes, Your Majesty.

Queenie And no food for a week.

Henchman Of course not, Your Majesty.

Queenie (*To herself*) When I catch that doctor, I'll put him on the rack and stretch him until he's nothing but a jigsaw.

Scene 6

Whitney's top-floor flat at White Tower, some days later

Whitney, Tom and Suzy are present.

Whitney   (*Putting down her mobile phone*) That was Dr Wright. He's set up a practice on the outskirts of the city, to look after the poor. What a good man he is.

Tom   You were right to warn him to keep away, though, for the time being at least. Queenie's Henchmen might be spying on him, hoping he'll lead her to you.

Whitney   Yes, you may be right; but it *is* a pity. I'd like to know him better. He saved my life.

Suzy   Just as you saved Tom's life.

Whitney   Oh, that was nothing. It's easy to fool a stupid Henchman. They may look tough on the outside, but they're as gooey as marshmallow inside. You just have to know how to handle them.

Tom   (*Laughs*) He's probably still standing out there trying to count to a hundred!

Suzy   (*Clicking the mouse on Whitney's computer*) Look at this e-mail, Whitney. It's one of your Granny-spies, isn't it?

Whitney   Yes. (*Reads from the screen*) "This is an urgent warning for Whitney. Queenie has discovered your whereabouts. The Henchmen are pouring out of Palace Tower in their cars. They're almost certainly coming to get you. You've got no more than ten minutes."

Ten minutes. Heavens! I hope it's enough time for me to escape.

Suzy   You stay right here, Whitney. The Henchmen haven't a chance of getting to you up here.

Whitney   How can you be so sure?

Tom   Every now and then they try and attack us, and each time we chase them away like a dog with its tail between its legs. We even enjoy their attacks.

Whitney   *Enjoy* them? What do you mean?

Suzy   Wait a minute. See what happens when I press this button. (*A siren wails*) That's the signal to activate the defence plan.

Whitney   What's the defence plan?

Tom   Well, for a start, we put string across every doorway, so the Henchmen trip up.

Suzy   We open up hidden mantraps in the entrance hall.

Tom   We put slippery liquid soap on the stairs.

Suzy   We let off stink bombs in the corridors.

Tom   We trail sticky webs down from the ceilings.

Suzy   We Super Glue the banisters.

Tom   And the lifts are filled with hideous, blood-curling cries . . .

Suzy   . . . which we recorded beforehand.

Whitney   Brilliant! This is something I want to see.

Narrator   As the Dwarfs predicted, the Henchmen didn't stand a chance. Before the day was out, the last bruised and battered Henchman was thrown howling into the mud outside.

Scene 7

Whitney's flat at White Tower, some days later

Narrator   The internal phone rang and Suzy answered it. It was Red and Wolfie – come to visit Whitney at her request. Once, when Red was a little girl, Wolfie was her enemy. But, being a brave girl, she sought him out, gave him some food, and they became firm friends. Now you couldn't part them. Funny how things turn out, isn't it?

Tom   Yes, Red's really nice. Brave, too. All the Grannies and War Widows adore her.

Suzy   But Wolfie's a bit . . . well, growly. He guards her night and day; he makes me quite nervous.

Red and Wolfie enter.

Whitney   I'm so glad to meet you, Red. Hello, Wolfie; you too. It was good of you both to come. I've been wanting to meet you.

Red   Any friend of the Dwarfs is a friend of mine. In times like these, friends should stick together, don't you think?

Whitney   Absolutely.

Red   What a wonderful flat! All white and chrome.

Suzy   Let me take your cloak and basket.

31

Tom	(*To Whitney*) Red spends much of her time taking spare food from the supermarkets to old Grannies and War Widows who can't get out or don't have enough money to feed themselves.
Red	There's so much hunger in the city now. Your stepmother –
Whitney	(*Sighing impatiently*) Yes, I'm sorry about her. And the Henchmen, do they leave you alone?
Red	So far, at least. (*Wolfie growls*) I'm harmless, I suppose. A do-gooder. But I'm getting worried now. There's something going on.
Suzy	What do you mean?
Red	Well, last night, several of my Grannies wouldn't answer their doors. They cowered behind them like frightened mice. That's not like them. Someone's got at them.
Whitney	And you think . . . ?
Red	I think it's the Henchmen's doing – on the orders of your stepmother.
Whitney	(*Angrily*) How dare she!
Red	I think she's demanding money from them. They all have nest-eggs, you see, under the beds and floorboards, because they don't trust the banks.

Whitney	Who would? Queenie controls them all now. It's a disgrace!
Red	And what's worse, two of my Grannies have disappeared. Their doors were broken down, their houses were ransacked, and no-one knows where they have gone.
Whitney	(*Hitting the table with her fist*) That woman! She's got to be stopped.
	Red*'s mobile telephone rings.*
Red	Hello? Goldie! What's the matter? What? Your shop's being ransacked? Henchmen! Hang in there, Goldie! I'm with the Dwarfs and Whitney right now. We're on our way.
Whitney	What's happening? Who's Goldie?
Red	She's my closest friend. She runs a locksmith's shop on Wilhelm Street. There's a sign above it which says: *Goldie Locks: Keep Those Henchmen at Bay* – you may have seen it. And now the Henchmen are attacking her.
Whitney	Whatever for?
Red	No time to explain. I must go and help her.
Whitney	I'm coming too.

Red   Are you sure?

Whitney Of course I'm sure. I've spent enough time
             skulking around here. It's time to strike back.
             Besides, the Dwarfs will see that no harm will
             come to me.

Scene 8

Goldie's shop

Narrator   Goldie, of course, as you've guessed, was once the famous house-breaker, Goldilocks, partial to eating porridge and breaking chairs. As a reformed character, she was soon advising on security, to keep the burglars *out*! A little later, Red and Wolfie arrived in their van outside Goldie's locksmith shop. Whitney and the Dwarfs followed on motorbikes. Henchmen were smashing up the shop.

Goldie   (*Shouting at **Henchman***) Put that teddy bear down at once!

Henchman   (*Laughs*) Like this? (*Stamping on it*)

Red   Do that again and Wolfie will bite your toes off!

Tom   If you don't all stop at once, we'll cover you with sticky webs.

Suzy   And we'll glue your feet with Super Glue.

Whitney   (*Shouts*) Stop now, or my Dwarfs will attack you! Remember what happened to you in White Tower? Well, this'll be ten times worse. You'll be trussed up like chickens and thrown into the river. It's your choice.

Goldie   Yes, get out of here. Go on. And don't you dare attack my shop again.

Henchman   (*To **Whitney**, shame-faced*) We was only doing our job. Your mother –

Whitney   (*Hisses*) She's not my mother. Now, get out of here. If you haven't gone by the time I've counted to ten . . . One, two, three, four, five –

Henchman   Scarper, lads. This one's almost as bad as the queen. It ain't worth the grief.

Narrator   The Henchmen half-bowed to Whitney, half-snarled at everyone else, edged back to their car and fled.

Red   Goldie, are you all right?

Goldie   Just *fuming*, that's all!

Whitney   (*To the **Dwarfs***) Right, everybody, help Goldie tidy up, OK?

Goldie   I'm so livid I can hardly talk, Your Majesty. You must forgive me.

Whitney   Call me Whitney. I was only too pleased to help. And I couldn't have done much without the Dwarfs.

Goldie   Well then, Whitney, I think you ought to know what's going on around here. Do you know what that charming stepmother of yours is demanding now?

Whitney   I dread to think.

Goldie   Half my takings! And if I don't give them to her
                each week, she'll set her Henchmen on to me, like
                she did tonight.

Red   You can be sure that this sort of thing is
                happening all over the city. It would explain
                why my Grannies won't open their doors to me;
                they're frightened it's the Henchmen knocking.

Whitney   (*Outraged*) She's gone too far this time.
                Something will have to be done about Queenie.
                What, I don't know yet. *But this can't go on.*

Scene 9

About the same time in Queenie's flat

Narrator   Queenie, too, was fuming. In the Surveillance Room, she had witnessed Red and Whitney's interference in her protection racket. Cunning as ever, she had an idea.

Queenie   (*To Maid*) Bring me Whitney's trunk – the one she keeps all her most precious things in.

Maid   I'm not sure which one that is, Your Majesty.

Queenie   Oh, don't give me that. The one she keeps hidden under the bed.

Maid   (*Pretending innocence*) Is there one there, Your Majesty?

Queenie   Don't play Little Innocent with me, girl. Of course there's one there, and I know what's in it. Fetch it at once.

Narrator   The maid hurried out. A few minutes later, two Henchmen carried in the trunk, then backed out sharpish.

Queenie   (*Rummaging around in the trunk*) What a lot of sentimental rubbish. I'd have had the whole lot thrown out if I didn't think it might come in useful. And I was right! Here it is, her precious silver comb. It once belonged to her dear, departed

mother. Yuk! Well, now, these sharp little
teeth won't just pierce the skin of her precious
little head, they'll pierce her precious little heart,
too . . . Now, what I need is a poison that doesn't
smell and can't be seen, and yet one prick of it will
do the job. Let me see . . . Ah, this one. I'll smear
a bit on the comb . . . That should do the trick.
Now, I'll wrap it up and send it to Whitney with a
note saying it's from a well-wisher. She'll never
guess it's from me!

Scene 10

Whitney's flat at White Tower, the next day

Narrator The deadly comb arrived and Whitney unwrapped it.

Whitney Oh, how wonderful! Someone at home has sent me my favourite comb. I've missed it so much. I expect it was my maid. She knew how much I treasured it.

Suzy Whitney, why is the comb so special?

Whitney (*Tearfully*) It once belonged to my mother. She used to comb my hair with it when I was a little girl, and sing songs to me while she did it. Those were my happiest times –

Tom Don't upset yourself.

Whitney I'll comb my hair and think of her . . . (*Runs the comb once through her hair*) Ouch! Whatever . . . ? Oh, the pain –

Tom (*Alarmed*) Whitney, what's the matter? What's happened?

Suzy (*Panicking*) She's passing out. Whitney, wake up.

Whitney (*Faintly*) Get Dr Wright. (*Falls*)

Tom She's passed out!

Narrator   There was pandemonium in the flat. It was full of wailing Dwarfs frightened that Whitney was dead. Dr Wright was called at once.

Doctor   Stand back, for goodness sake. Give the patient some air . . . Oh, Whitney, what has happened to you, you look so pale. Let me feel your pulse . . . She's alive! But the pulse is so faint, she's hovering between life and death. What happened to her?

Tom   She used this comb. It must have come from Queenie.

Doctor   Then it's bound to be poisoned. Heavens, I've got to find an antidote quickly. There's no time to lose.

Scene 11

At Palace Tower

Narrator   The next day, Queenie turned on her computer, expecting to be told that she was now the fairest of them all. She was outraged to discover that the answer was *still* Whitney Snow. In her rage, she had Red, Wolfie and Goldie arrested and slung into the dungeons at Palace Tower. Thankfully, things were looking a little better at White Tower.

Doctor   Well, Whitney, you're out of danger at last. It was touch and go for quite a while, but I felt sure you'd pull through.

Whitney   Once again, Doctor, you've saved my life. You're like a guardian angel. I don't know how to thank you.

Doctor   (*Modestly*) Just doing my job.

Tom   (*Bursting in*) Whitney! Red and Wolfie have been arrested. It's all over the city.

Suzy   (*Bursting in behind him*) And Goldie's been arrested too!

Whitney   Queenie! How dare she! This is the last straw. Something *has* to be done about her. Now!

Tom   We could use our catapults against them. Throw darts at them –

Whitney	No more games. We must use force against force. We must flush out my stepmother and her Henchmen from Palace Tower for good.
Suzy	But how?
Doctor	I've got it! The Grannies and War Widows. Queenie's really got them stirred up with her protection rackets. And now, by locking up Red, she's robbed them of their food supply. They'll be furious.
Tom	They're angry at Goldie's imprisonment, too. I've never seen them so stirred up.
Whitney	Then somehow we must harness all that anger and turn it against her.
Doctor	I'm sure all they're waiting for is a lead from you, Whitney. Now that Red and Goldie have been locked up, you're the only one they'll trust. And they know that you will be acting for the king and not your wicked stepmother. Strike while the iron is hot!
Whitney	Yes, you're right! Listen, I'll send them all an e-mail. Yes! A really stirring one, to get them out in the streets and marching on to Palace Tower.
Suzy and Tom	Yes, that's the way to do it!

Narrator   The message was a masterpiece. In ringing tones, it urged everyone to march on Palace Tower that evening, armed with any weapon they could find. And everyone who read it was roused to action. She signed it: Whitney Snow, Princess.

Scene 12

Palace Tower, that evening

Narrator	The maid and a Henchman were staring at the surveillance screens.
Henchman	I don't like the look of this. Have they all gone mad?
Maid	It's scary. Whatever's brought all these grizzled Grannies and wailing Widows out onto the streets?
Henchman	And just look at those terrifying brooms and sticks and mops.
Maid	(*Grimly*) You can bet they're heading this way.
Henchman	(*Nervously*) What, coming here?
Maid	Of course. Where else? And do you know why?
Henchman	No. Why?
Maid	You Henchmen are so dumb, aren't you? Queenie, of course. And all your bullying on her behalf.
Henchman	Who's that leading them on the motorbike, with a megaphone?
Maid	I bet that's Whitney under that crash helmet. Oh, boy, wait till Queenie hears about this!

Henchman   (*Scared*) Princess Whitney? Leading that lot? We don't stand a chance. I'm getting out of here.

Maid   Me too.

Narrator   The news soon spread through the Tower. Henchmen and maids, panicking at the approach of the motley army, fled Palace Tower like rats from a sinking ship. An hour later, Queenie, unaware of what was going on (for no-one dared tell her), was returning to her flat from the dungeons.

Queenie   I did enjoy myself this afternoon. Nothing like an hour or two taunting a wretched prisoner. Red's face! What a sight when I told her how we'd pluck the hairs from her mangy hound one by one until he was bald! Ha, ha! And Goldie's shriek when I said we'd put her precious teddies in the food mixer and make soup of them. I'm so imaginative, aren't I! Pity there's no-one here to appreciate it . . . Come to think of it, there *is* no-one here. No maid on duty. No Henchmen outside. Where are they? (*Screeches into her intercom*) MAIDS! GET HERE AT ONCE! . . . Where the devil are they? And why is everything so quiet? (*Into the intercom again*) HENCHMEN! GET HERE AT ONCE! (*There is still no answer*) If they've all gone out on some wretched seaside coach party behind my back, I'll have the Henchmen trampled upon and the maids boiled in oil. (*Listens*) What is that strange rumbling noise outside?

Narrator	She rushed to the window. There she saw the protest march.
Queenie	Aahhh! What the devil is that? Why are they all marching here? (*Into the intercom*) Henchmen, get here AT ONCE! (*There is no response*) The cowards. They've all fled. At the slightest sign of trouble . . . They've left me in the lurch. *How dare they!* And who is that leading that army of hags? Aahhh! It's Whitney Snow! My ungrateful stepdaughter. And those wretched Dwarfs. I might have known it.
Narrator	She howled and screamed and clawed the air. She rushed to her poisons and selected a tasteless, colourless poison. Calming down, she poured it into a jug of dragon-and-apple juice and placed the drink with some glasses on a tray in the lounge.
Queenie	It isn't over yet. I'll get even with that girl if it's the last thing I do. One sip of that and it'll burn her insides up. All their insides. Serves them right . . . But maybe it would be even more cunning to put the drink in the fridge. Yes! And I'll leave the glasses here, so as to put the idea of a drink into their heads. They'll never suspect it's poisoned then. (*Puts the drink into the fridge*) Not for nothing am I the most cunning of them all. Now, all I've got to do is wait . . . I'll hide in the big wardrobe.

Narrator	A few minutes later, Whitney, the doctor, Tom and Suzy arrived at Palace Tower. The crowd was not far behind.
Doctor	It seems strangely quiet in here.
Tom	The Henchmen will have scarpered at the first sign of trouble.
Suzy	Looks like the maids have scarpered too. What a panic there must have been!
Whitney	Before we go in, I want to say a word to the Grannies and War Widows. (*Turns and hushes the crowd*) My friends, you have been magnificent! You have struck terror into the hearts of the Henchmen and they have all fled. (*The crowd cheers*) Without them, the queen is helpless. We shall now go in and arrest her. Keep a careful watch for any stray Henchmen. From now on, you are free! (*More cheers*) No more hunger. No more fear. No more theft. (*More cheers*) I thank you from the bottom of my heart. And until my father returns from the Wars, I shall be in charge of the city. (*Huge cheers*)
Doctor	They really do love you, Whitney. I've never seen so much enthusiasm.
Whitney	Things will be different for them from now on. Come on, let's go inside. The first thing we must do is free Red, Goldie and Wolfie.

Narrator	It didn't take long to release their friends, especially as the Henchmen had left the keys.
Whitney	Red, Goldie, are you all right?
Red	We are now! It's fantastic to be free!
Whitney	Now we'll all go up and have it out with Queenie.
Doctor	If she's still here.
Whitney	Oh, I have a feeling she'll still be here. Her pride wouldn't let her flee like the others. She'll fight to the bitter end, like a cornered rat. Come on.
Narrator	But to their surprise, there was no sign of Queenie in her flat. They gave it a quick search but neglected to look in the wardrobe. When the others returned to the lounge, Wolfie alone continued the search.
Whitney	(*Disappointed*) She must have fled with the others after all.
Red	Then let's celebrate. You have won, Whitney. You have seized back your home and vanquished your wicked stepmother.
Whitney	Yes, let's. Look, there are some glasses here. She might even have some champagne in the fridge.
Suzy	I'll go and have a look.

Narrator	Suzy returned with the jug of dragon-and-apple juice.
Suzy	There was only this. But it looks quite nice – smells of apples.
Doctor	I suppose it'll have to do. I'll pour it.
Whitney	You know, Doctor, this drink makes me feel vaguely uneasy, and I don't know why.
Doctor	It smells delicious. Let's make a toast to –
Red	Wait a minute, Whitney. Wolfie's not here. He'd be hurt if we had a toast without him. Wolfie, where are you?
Tom	We left him in Queenie's bedroom. I think I can hear him growling.
Red	Listen! What's he yelping like that for? He's found something!
	Queenie *screams.*
Goldie	Goodness, what was that scream?
Narrator	There was another scream, so piercing that Whitney dropped her glass in surprise. To everyone's horror, the liquid hissed and steamed, burning a hole in the carpet.

Whitney	Queenie! How could I have been so stupid?
Doctor	(*Aghast*) She almost poisoned you again.
Goldie	(*In disbelief*) All of us.
Whitney	And this time it would have been lethal. What an evil heart she has.
Narrator	Wolfie dragged Queenie screaming into the lounge. With her dress in tatters, she looked a mess. She spat hate at them all.
Red	All right, Wolfie, you can put her down now. Good boy!
Whitney	(*Coldly*) Well, Stepmother, who is the fairest of them all now?
Queenie	You ungrateful child! I should have strangled you when you were a little brat.
Whitney	There'll be no more of that. Wolfie, you were wonderful. Now, take her down to the dungeons, will you?
Queenie	How dare you! Wretched girl! Let me go!
Red	Give her a taste of her own medicine.
Goldie	Put her in the one where the rats nibble your toes . . .

Red	. . . and the water drips on your head . . .
Goldie	. . . and the wind moans through the bars like a ghost.
Doctor	Sounds just the right treatment to me.
Suzy	And me.
Tom	She deserves a long stretch.
Queenie	You won't get away with this! Wait until the king gets home. I am his queen, remember. I'll see that he has the lot of you hanged.
Whitney	Oh no, you won't! When he hears about your poisons, your protection rackets, your attempts to kill me, you won't stand a chance. Now, take her away . . . No! Wait! I've got a better idea. Parade her through the city so that everyone can see how far she has fallen, how pathetic she looks. They can throw their rotten eggs and tomatoes at her. After that, she'll never be able to terrorise them again.
Narrator	Wolfie dragged Queenie away, assisted by Tom and Suzy. An hour later, Palace Tower was full of Grannies and War Widows, pretending to be Henchmen and maids, larking about with the Dwarfs. There was a party atmosphere. Whitney, Red, Goldie and Dr Wright were on the balcony, waving to the crowds dancing and carousing below.

Whitney   Until my father returns, this tower could become a little lonely. I hope, Red and Goldie, you'll come and stay with me? There's plenty of room.

Goldie   Of course we will, won't we, Red?

Red   We'd love to. But you know, Whitney, what this tower needs is Grannies in every apartment, where they can be safe and have lots of parties.

Goldie   And Dwarfs to keep them company and run their errands.

Doctor   (*Smiling*) And you'll need a doctor in residence.

Whitney   And a father home from the Wars. Welcome, everyone!

Christmas in the Other House

Judith O'Neill

Illustrated by Gerry Ball

In memory of Jean Kerr, who first gave me this story

Contents

Introduction

This play has been written as a stage play. It is set in a small town on the east coast of Scotland. Old Alec is looking back, as an old man, on an event that happened when he was a boy of twelve.

The action takes place in the kitchen/living-room of the house where Alec's grandparents lived when he was a boy. The kitchen and the stairs lie beyond this room, through a door at centre back of the stage. The room also has a door on one side, leading to the street, and another door on the opposite side, leading to the back garden.

Old Alec stands to one side of the stage, watching the action. When he is speaking, the other characters either freeze or silently act. When the other characters are speaking, Old Alec himself remains silent and still.

Not all the furniture that is carried about in the play need be real furniture, but there should be four real upright chairs and a table that are light and easy to move. Any other furniture could simply be large cut-outs, made from thick cardboard. One side could be painted black to represent Grandma's very old furniture, and the other side painted gold or yellow to represent Great-Aunt Ina's furniture. Or, more simply still, all the furniture except the four chairs and the table, could be imaginary, but carried slowly in and out as if everyone could see them plainly.

Characters

Old Alec   *Alec, as a man of 72*

Young Alec   *Alec, as a boy of 12*

Grandma (Jean)   *Alec's Grandma*

Grandpa (Col)   *Alec's Grandpa*

Great-Aunt Ina*   *Grandma's younger sister*

*Note: the 'I' in Ina is pronounced as in the word 'shine'

Scene 1

One Friday in October

Old Alec   There I am! That boy sitting at the table with his grandma and his grandpa. Or that's how I was! Sixty years ago when I was only twelve! I remember that day so clearly. It was the day that my Great-Aunt Ina arrived!

My mother and I lived in the same village as my grandparents, right on the edge of the sea. My mother wasn't well that year, so I spent a lot of time in my grandparents' house. Sometimes I even stayed the night. I used to sleep in a tiny attic bedroom that was more like a cupboard than a proper room. I loved that little room, tucked up snugly under the roof of my grandma's house.

There's my grandma! She's reading that letter from her sister Ina for the hundredth time. She's very upset. She's almost crying!

Grandma   Robert is dead! I just can't believe it! Oh, poor Ina! Poor Ina!

Grandpa   (*Patting **Grandma**'s hand*) There, there, Jean. Don't distress yourself, dear.

Grandma   But whatever will we do with her, Col? She's arriving *today*! Any minute now!

Grandpa	(*Holding **Grandma**'s hand*) Poor Ina's had a terrible shock, Jean, losing her husband so suddenly like that. Naturally, she wants to be with us here for a week or two. You'll be able to help her, dear.
Grandma	No, Col! You haven't read her letter properly. She doesn't say anything about a 'week or two'. She says she's sold her house and she's moving back to this village for good! That's *far* too quick! She should have taken more time before she decided. Poor Robert was only buried last week and she's sold up already!
Young Alec	But why is she moving down *here*, Grandma?
Grandma	She used to know the village well when she was a girl, Alec. She grew up with me in this very house, remember. She says the place is full of such happy memories of our childhood. So now poor Robert's dead, she wants to come back.
Young Alec	But where will she *live*?
Grandma	(*Glancing back at the letter*) She says she'd like to stay with us. I suppose that'll only be till she finds a nice place of her own. But the odd thing is, she's bringing all her furniture with her straight away.

Young Alec	Her furniture, Grandma? Why?
Grandma	She doesn't have any children, remember. I suppose she loves her furniture the way we love our children.
Young Alec	(*Smiling*) And your grandchildren!
Grandma	(*Smiling and nodding back to* **Young Alec**) Yes, dear. Probably she can't bear to be parted from her furniture even for a few weeks.
	Grandpa *walks across the room to look out of the door into the garden.*
Grandpa	Your grandma and I thought we could put your Great-Aunt Ina's furniture in the 'other house'. It won't be for long, will it, Jean? Just till she finds a place of her own.
Grandma	(*Laughing*) I suppose it's the best we can do, but Ina won't like the idea of her precious things going down to the other house.
Young Alec	(*Looking out to the garden*) Why do you always call it the 'other house'? It doesn't look anything like a house to me. It's only a tumbledown shed.

Grandma	It *was* a house once, dear. A hundred years ago! That's what my old grandfather told me. He always called it the 'other house', but even when I was a girl it wasn't really a house any more.
Young Alec	What was it?
Grandma	We just used it as a barn. It was stuffed full of hay for our horses. But then the winter storms made those great holes in the roof and the village boys broke all the windows.
Young Alec	But Grandma! Where will she sleep, this Great-Aunt Ina?
Grandma	I'm afraid she'll have to go up in the little attic bedroom, Alec.
Young Alec	(*Indignantly*) But that's *my* room! You know I always sleep there when I stay with you!
Grandma	You could just sleep here on the sofa by the fire. Or you could easily run back to your own warm bed at home. It's only along the street.
Young Alec	(*Angrily*) That's not fair, Grandma! You shouldn't give her *my* room!

Grandpa	Alec, Alec! Don't worry about where you'll sleep or where your Great-Aunt Ina will sleep. We'll sort all that out. (*Glancing up at the clock*) She'll be here any minute, Jean. Let's go out into the street to welcome her when she steps off that bus.
Grandma	Oh, Col! I feel so nervous!
Grandpa	(*Laughing as he puts his arm around* **Grandma**) You're still a bit scared of that younger sister of yours, aren't you, Jean? Don't you worry, dear. Everything'll be all right. We'll do our best to make her feel at home till she finds her own house, won't we, Alec?
Young Alec	(*Running to the street door*) The bus, Grandma! I can hear the bus!
	Grandma *and* **Grandpa** *hurry to the street door. They stand with* **Alec** *and look out into the street.*
Grandma	(*Softly, in admiration*) There she comes, Alec! That lady in the smart black coat and hat!
Young Alec	But her skin looks so smooth and young, Grandma!

Grandpa	And just look at her hair, Alec. Still not one touch of grey. Your Great-Aunt Ina's a fine-looking woman all right!
	Great-Aunt Ina appears in the doorway. Grandma rushes forwards and hugs her tight but Great-Aunt Ina stays stiff and upright.
Grandma	(*Nervously*) Dear Ina! We're so glad to see you! What a sad time you've been having!
Grandpa	(*Kissing Great-Aunt Ina on the cheek*) Ina! We're so very sorry to hear of your poor Robert's death. Come in! Come in! And here's young Alec waiting to welcome you too.
	Great-Aunt Ina comes into the room and looks down at Young Alec.
Great-Aunt Ina	So this is Alec!
	She bends stiffly and kisses Young Alec on the top of his head.
Great-Aunt Ina	(*Turning back to Grandma*) My furniture will be here tomorrow, Jean. I do hope you've made plenty of room for it!
Grandma	(*Gabbling anxiously*) Yes, yes, Ina. Col thinks it will be best if we put your things down in the other house.

Great-Aunt Ina   The other house! But that's just an old shed! My beautiful furniture can't go there.

Grandma   But Col's mended the roof already and he'll patch the broken windows this afternoon. And Alec will sweep the whole place clean for you, won't you, dear? Your furniture won't be there for long, aftcr all. You'll be wanting a nice place of your own soon, won't you, Ina?

Great-Aunt Ina   We'll just have to see, Jean. All in good time. All in good time.

Scene 2

The next day – Saturday

Grandma, Grandpa, Young Alec and **Great-Aunt Ina**
*stand clustered around the door into the garden. They are
watching as* **Great-Aunt Ina**'s *furniture and all her boxes
are carried through the room from the street door, out
through the garden door and down to the other house.*
Great-Aunt Ina *is excited and happy. She exclaims in
delight as she sees each familiar piece of furniture.*

Old Alec   (*Laughing gently*) I could hardly believe my
                      eyes that day when Great-Aunt Ina's
                      furniture was carried right through my
                      grandparents' garden and down to the other
                      house. Those poor removal men *staggered*
                      under the weight of it! I'd never *seen* such
                      furniture. So heavy and so splendid. So
                      shining and golden. Almost *yellow!* Nothing
                      like the dull old black of my grandma's
                      furniture. That golden colour is what I still
                      remember after all these years.

Great-Aunt Ina   My beautiful furniture! I do hope the men
                      will be careful with it. We don't want any
                      knocks or scratches, do we, Alec?

Young Alec   What a lovely colour it is, Auntie! There's
                      never been a table like that in our village.

Grandma	(*Muttering to* **Grandpa**) I don't like that yellow colour much, do you, dear?
Grandpa	(*Whispering*) Ugly, I'd call it. But we must be kind to poor Ina.
Great-Aunt Ina	(*Calling out loudly to the removal men in the garden*) Do be careful, men! That table's very valuable, you know. (*In a quieter voice, to* **Alec**) My chairs will be coming in a minute, Alec.
Young Alec	*All golden*, Auntie?
Great-Aunt Ina	Yes, all golden, Alec! That was the fashion when your great-uncle and I were married. Long years ago!
Young Alec	Your furniture's so beautiful!
Grandma	(*Quietly to* **Grandpa**) It still seems like new-fangled rubbish to me, Col!
Grandpa	(*Gently patting* **Grandma**'s *hand*) Our old black furniture will always look the best, Jean.
	Grandma *smiles at him and nods her head.*
Great-Aunt Ina	(*Speaking excitedly*) Here come the chairs now, Alec! (*Calling out loudly to the men*) Put those chairs around the table, men! My

armchairs will go each side of the fireplace. And just put my boxes on the floor by the table!

Young Alec   Auntie! You've got so many boxes! Whatever's inside them?

Great-Aunt Ina   All my precious treasures! Bits and pieces from my lovely old home in the north. Robert gave me such beautiful presents, every single birthday. I've kept them all, of course. (*Calling out to the men*) Thank you, men. That's the way! You're doing a good job.

Grandma   Well, Ina, I can't stand here all day, looking at your yellow furniture! I'd better get started on making the dinner. Now where's my apron? Ah, here it is.

Great-Aunt Ina   (*Interrupting*) No, no Jean! Now that I'm settled here I want to help you.

Grandma   There's no need for that, Ina.

Great-Aunt Ina   Just give me that apron and I'll make the dinner for us all. I'm sure I still remember where you keep your things.

Grandma   But I always enjoy cooking our meals.

Great-Aunt Ina   Jean, I insist! Now give me that apron!

Slowly, **Grandma** *takes off her apron and hands it over to* **Great-Aunt Ina**.

Grandma   Well, Ina, only this once.

Great-Aunt Ina   (*Putting on the apron*) There we are! That's better, isn't it? I'll just set this room to rights first.

Old Alec   All of us watched Great-Aunt Ina in silence as she tidied Grandma's room. She changed the position of two of Grandma's pictures on the walls. She moved one of Grandma's ornaments from the sideboard to the mantelpiece. Poor Grandma wiped away a few tears. I didn't understand why she was crying. I was only twelve years old, remember.

Great-Aunt Ina   Right, I'll get to work on our dinner this very minute. Jean, you just sit by the fire. You've been working hard all your life. You deserve a good, long rest!

Old Alec   Great-Aunt Ina certainly took charge of Grandma's kitchen! First she put the meat into the roasting tin and slid it into the hot oven. Then she peeled the potatoes. She chopped the carrots. All the time, she was humming happily to herself. But Grandma was restless. She wandered all around the room. Sometimes she timidly put her own things back in their right places, though she always made sure that Great-Aunt Ina was not watching her!

Grandpa	(*To **Alec**, in a loud whisper*) We're in for a wonderful treat today, Alec. Your Great-Aunt Ina is a splendid cook! Perhaps she'll offer to make our dinner every day! Then your dear grandma would never have to lift a finger again! (*Turning to **Grandma***) You'd love that dear, wouldn't you?
Grandma	(*Indignantly, in a loud whisper*) I certainly wouldn't love it at all. I want to be in charge in my own kitchen. That's only natural.
Old Alec	Two hours later, the meal was ready. The smell was wonderful! Great-Aunt Ina lifted the meat, the vegetables and the gravy onto the table. Then she sat at the head of the table. She was so happy!
Great-Aunt Ina	Come along, everyone! My great Saturday dinner is ready! A splendid leg of lamb! Poor Robert always loved a leg of lamb. I know you'll enjoy every mouthful.
	Grandma**, **Grandpa** and **Young Alec *take their seats at the table.*
Great-Aunt Ina	(*Turning to **Grandpa***) Now, Col, will you say grace?

All four bow their heads.

Grandpa   For what we are about to receive, may the
Lord make us truly thankful.

All   Amen.

*In silence, **Great-Aunt Ina** carves the meat
and serves the vegetables. She passes a full
plate to each person in turn. They start
eating.*

Grandpa   Wonderful, Ina! Truly wonderful! I was just
telling young Alec here what a marvellous
cook you are. You see what I meant now,
Alec, don't you?

***Young Alec** nods enthusiastically. **Grandpa**
eats quickly. **Grandma** picks sadly at her
food.*

Old Alec   My grandma seemed so sad that day, but I
didn't know why. Grandpa and I were taken
in too easily by Great-Aunt Ina! We just
couldn't see what she was doing to us.

Grandpa   What a wonderful meal, Ina! We've never
eaten anything so good, have we, Jean?

Grandma   (*Still picking at her food, her voice flat*)
No, we never have, Col. It certainly is
delicious.

Great-Aunt Ina	Well, Jean, I'll be glad to cook the dinner for you and Col every day.
Grandma	(*Protesting, wiping her tears from her eyes*) Not every day, Ina!
Great-Aunt Ina	It's the least I can do now I've come to live with you. Robert always said I was a good cook. He did love his food, my poor dear Robert!
Grandma	Please let me make some of the meals. The way I always do.
Great-Aunt Ina	No, no. You need your rest, Jean. I'll enjoy making your dinner every day. It's no trouble at all!

Grandpa rubs his hands together in delight. Young Alec smiles and nods at Grandpa.

Great-Aunt Ina	(*Briskly*) Now, Jean, tomorrow's Sunday, remember. I'll be going to church, of course. I know you don't bother about church, but I hope you make sure that young Alec here goes every Sunday.
Young Alec	(*Indignantly*) It's a three-mile walk to church, Auntie, and three miles back again! I never go!

Great-Aunt Ina	Three miles each way won't worry *me*, Alec, and they shouldn't worry you either! When I lived in Banff, I used to walk six miles to church. Now, Jean, about tomorrow's dinner.
Grandma	I always cook a good Sunday dinner, Ina, and I'll cook it tomorrow as usual!
Great-Aunt Ina	No, no, Jean! I don't like to see people working on Sunday. It's the day of rest. So we'll just eat cold meat from this fine leg of lamb. I'll prepare the vegetables this afternoon so you'll only have to put them on to boil tomorrow, just before I get back from church.
Grandma	(*Meekly*) Perhaps I could just make a nice Sunday pudding, Ina?
Great-Aunt Ina	No need at all, Jean!
Grandma	Col does love my puddings.
Great-Aunt Ina	This big apple pie I've made for our dinner today will easily do us for another meal. I'll just heat it up again tomorrow. All right?

Great-Aunt Ina hums cheerfully to herself as she clears away the dirty dishes.

Grandma   (*Quietly but angrily*) Col! Now I'm not even allowed to make my nice Sunday pudding!

Great-Aunt Ina puts the apple pie on the table in front of her place and sits again.

Great-Aunt Ina   (*Triumphantly*) Now then, apple pie everyone? Alec dear, you can pass the cream.

Scene 3

A week later – Sunday

Young Alec and Grandpa sit by the fire. Young Alec is reading the property section of the local newspaper. Grandma has her apron on and is bustling about, setting the table and singing to herself. She is happy again.

Old Alec   (*Chuckling to himself*) While the cat's away the mice do play! Great-Aunt Ina is not back from church yet, so Grandma has the kitchen to herself again. It's been a whole week since she's been allowed to go in there and she's certainly making the most of it. She's put the vegetables on to boil and she's even made a cake!

Grandma   (*To herself*) Ina will soon be home. My cake must be almost ready. I'll just have a peep. (*She opens the oven door and looks in at the cake*) Mmm! That smells good! (*She shuts the oven door*) I can hear Ina's footsteps coming up the path already. Now I'll strain those vegetables. (*She carries one saucepan of vegetables towards the sink*) Oh, here she is!

Great-Aunt Ina   (*Taking off her coat and talking all the time*) Here I am, Jean. Back in good time. Don't you bother with those carrots. I'll take over now. We had such a good sermon from the minister! 'By their works shall ye know them!' That was his text. (*Suddenly startled*) Jean! Whatever's that strange smell?

Grandma (*Sniffing the air*) I can't smell anything, Ina. Just the potatoes and the carrots. They're all beautifully cooked.

Great-Aunt Ina Something sweet, Jean. Something in the oven perhaps? (*She flings open the oven door and peers inside. She speaks in horror.*) A cake, Jean! You've gone and made a cake! And on a Sunday too. Whatever were you thinking of?

Grandma (*Timidly*) It only took me a minute, Ina. (*Now in a stronger voice*) Surely I can make a cake in my own kitchen!

Great-Aunt Ina There's no need for you to be making cakes at all, Jean. *I'm* here to help you now. You just sit down by the warm fire and I'll take your cake out of the oven when it's ready. Not that we really need a cake on the Sabbath!

 Grandma takes off her apron. She sinks into a chair by the fire. **Great-Aunt Ina** *bustles about, putting cold meat and hot vegetables on the table.*

Young Alec (*Waving his newspaper excitedly*) Auntie! Look here in yesterday's paper!

Great-Aunt Ina	What is it, Alec?
Young Alec	There's a lovely little cottage for sale right in our own village.
Great-Aunt Ina	Oh, it's far too soon for me to be thinking of buying a cottage.
Young Alec	But it might suit you, Auntie.
Great-Aunt Ina	No thanks, Alec. I'll need to take my time.
Young Alec	Well, here's another one, Auntie. It's in the town, right next to the church.
Great-Aunt Ina	No thanks, Alec.
Young Alec	But you wouldn't have that long walk every Sunday.
Great-Aunt Ina	Your dear grandma needs my help in this kitchen every day. How could I help her if I lived three miles away in the town?
Grandpa	You're quite right, Ina. We all need you here. (*Turning to **Grandma***) We've never eaten so well in our whole life, have we dear? (*Turning back to **Ina***) Ina, you really are the best cook in the world.

***Great-Aunt Ina** smiles in triumph.*

Grandma	(*Sharply in an undertone to* **Grandpa**) You always used to say that I was the best cook in the world, Col. You seem to have forgotten!
Old Alec	Yes, he really does seem to have forgotten all those wonderful meals my grandma made for him through fifty years of marriage. Whatever's happened to him?
Great-Aunt Ina	Sit up, everyone! My Sunday dinner's ready!

All four take their seats at the table and bow their heads.

Scene 4

Two months later – two days before Christmas

*The four sit in exactly the same position, just finishing a meal. **Old Alec** is watching the four at the table.*

Old Alec   Two months have passed. Great-Aunt Ina has cooked us a wonderful dinner every single day since she arrived. Grandpa and I loved her meals, but Grandma never quite seemed her old self after Auntie moved in. She ate all the marvellous dinners, of course, but she didn't say much about them. It was a mystery to me. I thought she'd be so glad to sit by the fire and let her sister do all the hard work.

Grandpa   (*Putting down his knife and fork and sitting back in his chair*) Another triumph, Ina!

Young Alec   Wonderful, Auntie!

Great-Aunt Ina   (*Smiling at **Alec**, then turning to **Grandma***) Jean, I was just thinking. This table of yours is a poor old thing, isn't it?

Grandma   A poor old thing?

Great-Aunt Ina   Christmas is only two days off and we really need a decent table for our Christmas dinner, don't we?

Grandma	(*Shocked*) But my table *is* decent, Ina! It belonged to our own dear mother. Don't you remember?
Great-Aunt Ina	Of course I remember, Jean. She was a good woman, our mother, but she had very old-fashioned ideas about furniture. Let's bring my nice table up from the other house. Robert was always so fond of it. It will be just right for Christmas.
Grandma	I'm not sure, Ina. I'm not sure at all.
Great-Aunt Ina	And while we're about it, we might as well bring the chairs too. Your old chairs could go down in the other house with your table. They'd be quite safe there. Come on, Col! And you too, Alec! We'll do it this very minute. Just help me lift this poor old table!
Old Alec	Yes, I helped her. I have to admit it. I didn't understand what I was doing. Grandpa hesitated for a second, but then he helped her too. We carried Grandma's old table and chairs right down to the other house and then we brought Ina's fine *golden* table and chairs to take their place.
	*As **Old Alec** talks, **Grandma** walks from table to fire. **Grandpa** and **Young Alec** carry the table and chairs out of the room. Then they come in again with **Great-Aunt Ina's***

chairs and table. **Grandma** *sits crouched over the fire throughout, not even looking up.*

Great-Aunt Ina (*Gazing happily at her table*) That looks much better! Thank you, Alec, and you too, Col. I'll just give my table a good polish. That's all it needs.

Great-Aunt Ina sets to work, polishing her table of golden wood. **Grandpa** *and* **Alec** *watch her in silence. As she polishes she hums or sings an old-fashioned hymn such as 'Fight the good fight' or 'What a friend we have in Jesus'.*

Great-Aunt Ina There we are, Jean! All ready for Christmas on Monday! You must admit that my table looks much better than your poor old thing.

Grandma (*Angrily*) No, Ina! I admit no such thing! My dear old table belongs in this room! It's been at home in this house ever since our mother came to live here as a young bride. I'll just go down to the other house and make sure it's all right.

Great-Aunt Ina laughs. **Grandma** *hurries from the room, out into the garden.*

Great-Aunt Ina Now I'll polish the chairs. You can help me, Alec, and you too, Col. Here's a cloth for each of you. Many hands make light work!

The three of them polish the chairs with enthusiasm.

Great-Aunt Ina   (*As they polish*) We might as well finish off the job properly, Col. Let's bring up my nice wardrobe and my chest of drawers and my bed. I do love to have all my own things around me at Christmas. The bedroom's very small but we'll fit everything in somehow. But first we'll run up to the bedroom and carry all your poor old bits and pieces down to the other house.

Grandpa   (*Alarmed*) Are you quite sure, Ina?

Great-Aunt Ina   Of course I'm sure! Hurry up, Col! I can't carry all that stuff by myself!

Grandpa   Come on then, Alec. Lend a hand. Your auntie does have some beautiful furniture, doesn't she?

Young Alec   (*Whispering*) I don't think Grandma will like it, Grandpa.

Grandpa   She'll soon get used to the change, Alec. Come upstairs and we'll make a start on the old wardrobe. We'll probably have to take it to pieces.

Great-Aunt Ina   (*Happily*) Thanks so much, Col!

Grandpa goes into the kitchen. Then his feet are heard on the stairs. Young Alec pauses at the door into the kitchen, looking back over his shoulder.

Young Alec   (*Worried*) But where's Grandma, Auntie?

Great-Aunt Ina   (*Laughing*) Oh, she's still down at the other house, looking in through the window. I don't know why she doesn't come to help us. Thank goodness it's Sunday tomorrow and Christmas Eve as well. We can all have a good rest.

Sounds are heard of the old wardrobe being taken to pieces upstairs. Great-Aunt Ina goes on polishing her table and chairs. She stil hums the same hymn happily to herself.

Scene 5

Sunday – Christmas Eve

Midday. The table is already set for the meal.
Grandma, **Grandpa** and **Young Alec** *sit close by the fire.*
They are completely still.

Old Alec
Christmas Eve! It happens to fall on a Sunday, so Great-Aunt Ina is still away at church, of course. The whole house feels peaceful. But something's the matter with poor Grandma. Just look at her. She's put the vegetables on to boil exactly as Auntie had told her to do, and she's sitting by the fire, but she's not happy, is she? Look at those tears in her eyes. Look at those twisting hands. I just couldn't understand it at the time. I didn't know what was the matter with her. But now I see how angry she must have felt. Her sister was taking over the whole house.

Grandma
(*Leaping suddenly to her feet*) I can't bear this a minute more, Col! I'm going to move all my furniture back into my own house this very minute!

Grandpa
(*Alarmed*) No, no, dear! Don't do that! You'll strain your back! And we mustn't annoy Ina, whatever we do. After all, she won't be with us much longer, will she? It's only till she finds herself a house.

Grandma	She's been here for two months already, Col, and she hasn't even started looking for a house! (*Turning to **Young Alec***) Alec, will you help me?
Young Alec	She'll be furious, Grandma!
Grandma	Who cares? Come on, Alec! If your grandpa won't help, we'll do it by ourselves!
Grandpa	Oh, all right then, I'll lend you a hand. But I warn you, Jean, Ina will be angry!
Old Alec	I had to help them, of course, but I was really scared. First we took Great-Aunt Ina's table down through the garden to the other house and we brought Grandma's table back again. Then we took out all the golden chairs and carried in the black chairs. We worked so fast that we were almost running! Then Grandma put her own old pictures on the walls again, her old cloth on the table, and her old ornaments on the mantelpiece. She kept on singing a hymn that she'd always loved: 'Onward Christian soldiers, marching as to war.' I couldn't help smiling to myself. It really was a kind of war! I was wildly excited at what we were doing, but I was frightened too. Great-Aunt Ina would be back from church any minute. Whatever would she say when she saw what we had done?

Grandma	(*Smiling as she surveys the room*) Right! That looks much better! Let's sit by the fire.

*The three of them sit huddled nervously over the fire, waiting for **Great-Aunt Ina** to return from church.*

Young Alec	Here she comes, Grandma! I can hear her footsteps in the street. I'm scared!

***Grandma** takes his hand and squeezes it. **Great-Aunt Ina** opens the street door and comes into the room, dressed in her smart black coat and hat. She looks quickly around the room. She stands still for a minute as she realises what has happened, but she pretends not to notice. Then she speaks brightly.*

Great-Aunt Ina	Here I am, back again! Thank you so much, Jean, for cooking those vegetables for me. I'll soon have everything ready, so come to the table straight away.
Old Alec	We took our places nervously while Great-Aunt Ina strained the vegetables, put them into serving dishes and set them on the table. Then we watched in complete silence as she carved the cold roast meat and served everything onto our plates. We all felt so guilty. But Auntie didn't say a word about the furniture. She seemed so bright and cheerful

that I really wondered if she'd noticed what we'd done. Surely she couldn't have missed it. But why was she pretending?

Great-Aunt Ina   Well, Christmas Day tomorrow! Alec, it's a pity your dear mother still isn't quite well enough to come here with you. But I'll be sure to take some dinner along to her later in the day. I know she'll love it. I've made a *wonderful* pudding, stuffed with raisins and sultanas! Now, heads bowed, everyone! (*All bow their heads*) Col, you say grace!

Grandpa   For what we are about to receive, may the Lord make us truly thankful.

All   Amen.

Young Alec   (*In a stage whisper to* **Grandma**) Grandma! I don't think Auntie's noticed anything yet!

Old Alec   But she'd noticed all right!

Scene 6

Christmas Day

Grandma and Grandpa sit close to the fire.
They look depressed. Great-Aunt Ina is busy cooking.
Young Alec bursts in through the door, laden with
presents and balloons.

Old Alec   I still remember the terrible shock I felt as I rushed into that room on Christmas Day. The table was completely bare! Where was the snowy white tablecloth? Where was the food? Where were all the presents?

Young Alec   (*Gasping in shock as he sees the empty table*) Here I am, Grandma! Mother's a bit better today. She's really looking forward to seeing you this afternoon. Happy Christmas, everyone! I've got presents for you all! (*Puzzled, he stares at the bare table*) I do hope I'm not too early, Auntie.

Great-Aunt Ina   (*Smiling as she puts on a heavy coat and hat*) No, you're not too early, Alec dear. Everything's ready. We're going to eat our Christmas dinner in the other house today. My lovely table is all set down there and we only have to carry the food through the garden. You can help me, Alec.

Young Alec	But, Auntie, it's so cold down there! We'll be frozen to death!
Great-Aunt Ina	You can just keep your coat on, dear. That's what I'm doing. A good Christmas dinner deserves a good table, you know. We'll come back here to the fire after we've eaten our pudding.
Grandma	(*Indignantly*) Well *I'm* not going down to the other house! This is *my* home, Ina, and *my* warm fire. This is the right place to eat our Christmas dinner, sitting around my own old table!
Grandpa	Yes, Ina. Let's have our Christmas dinner here by the fire, just the way we always do.
Old Alec	But Great-Aunt Ina took the Christmas dinner from the oven and carried it out through the back door. Then she came back for the vegetables and the gravy.
Young Alec	(*Whispering to* **Grandpa**) I think she really is taking our dinner to the other house.
Grandpa	Come on, Alec. Let's go and talk to her.
	***Grandpa** and **Young Alec** go to stand just inside the garden door. They look out into the garden. **Grandma** stays by the fire, holding her hands to the warmth.*

Young Alec	(*Exclaiming in delight*) Look, Grandpa! It's snowing! A white Christmas!
Great-Aunt Ina	(*Calling from the garden*) Everything's ready, Col! Come on! And you too, Alec! Your Christmas dinner is waiting for you on my beautiful table!
Grandpa	She keeps on calling. She keeps on calling. I really must go. Poor Ina, she has no-one left in the world since Robert died. Yes, I must go!
	He steps out through the doorway, but then turns and steps back in again.
Grandpa	No, no! I can't go. It's not right at all. I can't leave Jean here on her own.
	*He walks back to the fire again. He sits down beside **Grandma** and takes her hand in his. At the same time, **Young Alec** pulls his coat tighter, picks up his cap from a chair and puts it on.*
Great-Aunt Ina	(*Calling loudly from the garden, more urgently now*) Alec! Alec! I'm waiting for you! As long as you live, you'll never eat a Christmas dinner as good as this one!
Grandma	(*Calling gently to Alec*) Come back to the fire, Alec dear. There's plenty of good bread

and cheese in the cupboard. We won't go hungry.

Young Alec looks back at his grandparents by the fire, but then makes up his mind. He steps out through the door and disappears from sight.

Great-Aunt Ina (*Calling from off stage, triumphantly*) Good boy, Alec! Good boy!

We still hear her happy, clear voice from the other house.

Great-Aunt Ina That's my boy! Now you sit here on one side of my lovely table and I'll sit on the other side. That's the way! Now I'll say grace. Bow your head, Alec. Good boy! For what we are about to receive, may the Lord make us truly thankful. Amen. There we are! Now eat up, Alec! Eat up! That's my boy!

*Off stage, loud sound of **Young Alec** jumping to his feet and his chair falling over. We hear him spitting food out of his mouth. **Great-Aunt Ina**'s voice changes suddenly from triumph to alarm.*

Great-Aunt Ina (*Angrily*) Alec! Alec! Whatever are you doing? Don't spit that good food on the floor! Where are you going? Alec! (*Her voice breaking into a cry of despair and grief*)

	Come back to the other house, Alec. Come back! Come back!
Old Alec	I flung myself into Grandma's arms. She hugged me tight. I couldn't hold back my tears now. I was sobbing and sobbing!
Young Alec	Grandma! Grandma! I didn't eat it, Grandma! I didn't eat it!
Grandma	Good boy! Good boy!
	Great-Aunt Ina *appears, standing just outside the garden door. She is crying.*
Great-Aunt Ina	(*Holding out her arms towards* ***Alec*** *and sobbing wildly in grief*) Come back, Alec! Come back! You can't leave me all alone in the other house! You can't leave me alone in the other house on Christmas Day!
	Alec *glances up at her, but then turns back to* ***Grandma*** *and stays with his arms around her.*
Old Alec	Three days later, Great-Aunt Ina found a place of her own in town. I hardly ever saw her again. But after all these years I still can't forget that terrible look of grief on her face as I left her there, alone in the other house, on Christmas Day.